Presented to:
Joyce Littleton Bass

Presented by:
Razors & Bandaid Poetry Guild

Date:
March 17, 2008

Joyce,
Hope you enjoy the poems!
C. Meredith

Joyce,
To God Be the Glory for the Things He Has done!!
B. DeLoach Presley

Joyce,
I hope you enjoy reading each of the poems. May God bless.
Williefene S. Ford

Razors & Bandaids
presents
Guaranteed To Cut & Soothe

Bloomington, IN Milton Keynes, UK

AuthorHouse™
1663 Liberty Drive, Suite 200
Bloomington, IN 47403
www.authorhouse.com
Phone: 1-800-839-8640

AuthorHouse™ UK Ltd.
500 Avebury Boulevard
Central Milton Keynes, MK9 2BE
www.authorhouse.co.uk
Phone: 08001974150

© 2006 Razors and Bandaids. All rights reserved.

No part of this book may be reproduced, stored in a retrieval system, or transmitted by any means without the written permission of the author.

First published by AuthorHouse 9/13/2006

ISBN: 1-4259-5304-2 (sc)
ISBN: 1-4259-5305-0 (dj)

Library of Congress Control Number: 2006907234

Printed in the United States of America
Bloomington, Indiana

This book is printed on acid-free paper.

INTRODUCTION

(This poem is submitted as a poetic introduction to our first volume of poetry)

"The Birth of our Guild -- Razors & Bandaids"

One spring evening two minds intermingled on the idea of local poets
intertwining and sharing the music of their hearts
So strong was the bonding that it branched out and materialized
only after the two intertwined with another two or three
who understood the plan and tended to agree.
Five charter members came together to form this guild
To work together and ultimately build
a club for poets to meet and greet
and read and discuss and critique and eat!
They knew that the guild must be called on by name
So some got involved in a kind of a game
"Razors and Bandaids" was the name that stood out
The perfect name, there was no doubt!!
Perhaps you wonder how this name caught our eye
Without resistance, I'll tell you why
It's simply because:
Some poems like razors cut deep to the core
But some like bandaids help to heal a sore.
So "Razors & Bandaids" suddenly came into being
With words, ideas, meters and rhythms fleeing
Out of five hearts came the music of the soul
Two men, three women with stories untold
Thus the birth of our guild -- a blessing for each
A volume of poetry -- within our reach.

--Bettye DeLoach Presley

TABLE OF CONTENTS

JOSH EDWARD JOHNSON, Sr.

WGLY (Double You Ugly)	3
Echoes of False Love	4
Blacklight	5
Circles & Squares	6
Addiction	7
Words	8
Beauty Part I "sweet"	9
Finally Back Home	10
Song for our Country	11
Abstractly Nothing	12
I Want to be the One	13
Education	14
Early Morning Love	15

BETTYE DELOACH PRESLEY

Back in the Day	19
... But We Got Game	22
Damn, Dam	23
A Formal Thank You	24
Minds Gone Awry	26
In His Likeness	27
Here's to the Red, Black and Green !!!	28
But Was It Ever Really Lost?	29
Sweet Solace	30
An Addict's Plea	33

The Absence of Light	34
Within	35
Mystified!!!	36
The Magic of Words	37
Take A Closer Look, Please	38
Visions	40

DEBRA ANN JASPER

My Sleepless Dream	43
I Want Love	44
Can Love Be Trusted?	45
The Fall	46
He'll Do It	47
Oh, Katrina	48
It Doesn't Matter	49
My Soul As A Lookout	50
Things I Like In People	51
First Lady Rosa Parks	52
You Just Can't Tell	53
A Prayer To My Father	54
Poetry To The Poet	55
Dna	56
The Eyes of a Child: Innocent Eyes	58
Evolving Love	61

CHARLES MEREDITH

Take This As A Lovepoem	65
A Ruck Of This And That	66

I Love To Love	67
A Saintified Church Meetin In Lakeport, Arkansas	68
After Hearing The Call For Participants In The Million-man March	69
For You Maurice, To Read When You Can	70
Poeticnotions	72
Sharing Forever	74
For A Daddy Who Straightway Ran To A Bigger Place And More Space	75
I Expect To See Him	76
Beauty And The Beholder	77
Conductor Of The Chinaman-store Bench	78
You Know, I've Never Read A Marriage Poem	79
Across The Tracks, On Armstrong Street	80
I Think You Should Pull Your Hair Straight Back	82

WILLIEFENE SYKES FORD

Rebuttal	85
Wise Up, Black Man	86
Psychotic Intoxication	87
Mesmerized	88
Weak Women	89
The Gambler	90
We Need To …	91
Despite the Facts	92
Don't Ask Me to Leave	93
A Dead Slave's Prayerful Confession	94
I Can't Call It!	96
Vain Labour	97

No Friends	98
I Praise the Man	99
The Men Of This World	100
From the Side of the Road	102
The Struggles Of The Real Poet	104
Don't Give Up, Yet	106
It's Gone!!	107

JOSH EDWARD JOHNSON, Sr.

Wgly
(Double you ugly)

Imaginations could not preceive dimensions
    stretched 'way pass known degrees
if dissected strand for strand dominion by dominion would
    bewilder astound & astonish intellectual brain cells
that overload nerves whose wet endings have
    been battered & battered & battered.
Still the band played on and so did it rain
    flooding, flooding, flooding,
flooding sewers running over caskets
    popping up pipelines busting.
Have you ever seen a tree tear out of the ground
    & fly for a minute or two or three?
Somewhere a little bit above the Cape of Good Hope
    northwest side off shore
a massive herd of killer whales corraled a giant pool of plankton
at the same time
nearby on land a mass metamorphosis of hercules
    moths flapped for the first time
plus the hummingbirds hummed & hummed   humming
to a tune of one hundred twenty-five miles per hour
    once it got it to me.
Now I gotta wade water if I go anywhere
    I want to, but I can't stay here
no power nothing's open   was that a cottonmouth
    mocccasin or a baby alligator............
with higher ground on my mind having no choice but to move
got shipped to Memphis where finally being made comfortable
half 'way thru my first brew it hit me
this is just one thought
what about the rest of 'em?

Echoes of False Love

Echoes of false love float up to the sky
unnoticed, unheard, only to die.
Clouds fogging memories,
shielding the past,
solid love still dissolving the spell that was cast.
Echoes of false love silently fade,
breaking strong bonds and plans that were made.
An unfinished painting that could have come true,
now uncontrasting colors all tainted with blue.
Echoes of false love, where do they go?
Why do they come? I'd like to know!
In places for heartaches and dried up tears,
go echoes of false love as true love appears.
Echoes of false love never tell why
the kisses and "I love you's" had to die.
But they do fade away leaving you lonely and blue
And the only cure is a love that's true!

Blacklight

Twas a blacklight on the darkest night
That showed the way to hell
And as they blazed their way
the last to stay
forever sealed the trail.
Was a blacklight on the blackest night
That overpowered the gun
and when daylight came so tender and tame
That light became the sun.
Once there was a lie
All across the sky
And those who knew were few
But the clouds had to yield
to the lights' will
now truth is shining through.
The new day was clear
For the night had banned fear
And love regained her place on the throne
Plus with harmony and peace
Overtaking the east
On the moon its reflection shone.
Now all blacklight people are out of hell
But the devil is still around
So we must walk in the light
Keeping to the right
Remembering silence is the greatest sound
Keep your head up high
Tune to the sky
Don't let your feet be misled
Since we're out of hell
We might as well
See to it the devil is dead.

Circles & Squares

Believe me you can tell me the meaning of your poem
BUT
if it does not say it
only you & me understand it
unless you say it with flare touching that emotion we all
recognize as fact
then we understand
BUT
if it don't rhyme & its supposed to
don't make any sense 'fo too long & I'm thru
what I cannot understand
is a waste of my time
reading this I can easily direct your train of thought
down a smooth road or into a brick wall
but to nowhere
for nothing
if the words spoken don't match
don't ask me if it was good
don't ask me anything about it
just do what you call poetry
and perhaps
one of us who does know how to do it
will show you how!

Addiction

I light you up
Oh, snake that you are
To fill my lungs with nicotine and tar
And though I know the story, oh so well
I'd bum a smoke off the devil

If I wind up in hell!!

Words

Words will make you love
Words will make you hate
Words are even potent enough
to change a person's fate.

Strong words, weak words, promises, lies
will all educate and make you wise.
Your words, my words, bad words, good
Do you use your words as you should?
Words can kill or make you live.
How do you compare with the words you give?
Some people's words divide them into thirds
'cause with them
words are words are words
without any action
ain't nothing but words.
In knowing that words are words again,
it's all what you do with your words, my friend!

Beauty
Part I "sweet"

It's in the eyes of the beholder -- a sunlit ray
from the words of a poet knowing just what to say.
an artistic rendition of a place in the mind;
the ability to see where others are blind.
It's a confident walk -- a ball that wet the net
powder dry to some -- to others sweat
beads of jewelry -- the clinking of coin
you know I wanted to -- they asked me to join
Nine miles away -- a seat up front
I say frank -- you think blunt
thinking about a good time -- knowing it was duty
of all the words that come to mind -- I say "beauty"!

Finally Back Home

A lot of folks ain't coming back home to the places they used to roam.
'cause where they used to roam ain't there no more!
You don't have to believe me 'cause I told you so.
I ain't never seen nothing like this in all of my life...
energy so thick, slicing like a knife.
ripping the tops off of big buildings, trees uprooted
what the thugs didn't get -- nature looted!
ain't no tumbleweeds blowing, still it's like a ghost town.
everybody here working come from higher ground
I got people shipped to Texas said they got their "big mac".
ain't no might return, say they ain't coming back!
I saw one brother on clean up and thought it silly
all else doing it speak spanish or hillbilly
Nineth Ward is no more, but the playing field is level.
Eastover looks like it had a visit from the devil.
Poor people and well to do same problem where to stay
few churches fewer people know they need to pray
They say in a couple of years all will be alright
but that's what they see, 'cause it aint in my sight
To get everybody back, it would take a subpoena
in this horrific aftermath of what we call Katrina.

Song for our Country

America, to you this song we sing
From sea to sea let freedom ring
The blood, the sweat and all the tears
Let freedom ring two hundred years.
To you, America, we sing our song
Let every heart move every tongue
The home of the brave, the land of the free
Equality, justice and liberty!
An idea started two hundred years ago
And will continue for two hundred more.
Giving we the people the controlling voice.
Though it's imperfect, it's still our choice.
Our father, our mother, our sister, our brother
Whoever you are, whatever your color.
Americans love America, our country 'tis of thee
Though opinions differ, on this we all agree.
Through the good and bad times all across this land
Ole Glory still waves her lovely hand.
So let's sing for our country and sing out loud!
Lift every voice, show that you're proud.
Sing with a feeling and words that are true.
America, we americans do love you!

Abstractly Nothing

The cat scrawled on the wall;
The die will turn
Where's there's too much friction, something will burn.
Day turns into night, night into day.
The wise ole owl knows it's okay.
Summer, Fall, Winter, Spring
Snow in July doesn't mean a thing.
Lightning claps and thunders flash
I overheard her say "You know you talk plenty trash."
Snakes and wolves close in for the kill.
No one listens to the fool on the hill.
Through the dust and the smoke, the opening is clear
Up and down the back a chill is frozen by fear.
Screams and shouts yell to be heard
And I, my friend, have not said a word.
To make the claim
the game,
the aim,
The blame, the same
the rules, the name.
A star can't really out shine the sun.
Check out where I'm coming from.

I Want to be the One

I want to be the one you would give the time
Coming from my heart though these words may rhyme
I would say and do for you to understand
Plain and simple I want to be your man.
I want to be the one to share your dream
Every aspect, you know what I mean
Critique your makeup, wash the dishes
Homes and cars, toys and switches
With the most respect I admire your body
The way you'd pout if I were tardy
In this bittersweet world, you are sweet
With you in my life, I would be complete
Your face, your hair, the way you carry yourself
On my checklist there's nothing left.
Perfect score, I pray I measure up to half
I'd be embarassed if at you you'd laugh
'cause if given the chance I could ace your world
be your boy and you be my girl
man and woman, husband and wife
I want to be around you all of my life
I hope I'm not keeping you too long
But these feelings I have are oh so strong
Eye to eye, I'm the first to let you know I've got a crush
Only between you and me does it mean that much?
I want to be... I'm gonna be the one to let you know
I'd be doing me wrong if I didn't so
Nothing beats a failure but a try
And so to you I will not lie
Excuse me Madam, do you have the time?
You look a million; I feel like a dime
See, I wrote this poem and every word is true
I'd like you to hear it, 'cause its for you
I want to be the one ...

Education

At the end of the last bell
materialistic minds bent on buying life
exist in cube shaped worlds
above and beneath the Earth
Silently praying to green and silver Gods
to grant their wishes
for an Aladdin's lamp of their own.

In the meantime, they teach
Philosophy classes
dealing with thousand year old eyes
that justify immoral acts of History
and make good topics for Sociology.

After a high getting smoke break
took all the time from P. E.,
proving x-y='s
You're gonna miss English just this time.
Searching, researching, finding facts
"And that will be all for today, Class."
"Don't forget to study your notes
and have your assignments ready for tomorrow."

Outside in front of the Student Union Building,
a crowd is gathering listening to a brother shout.
"And if we don't get that, Class,
I ask you "Why?" "According to who?"
and "In the name of what?"
"I say, we don't know enough about ourselves
and if we don't get the knowledge,
we will never know.

"Wake up, my people, there's a job to be done!"
Wake up: and I woke up
thirty minutes late for Speech
and as I turned over slowly, I realized
This is going to be one of my "forget it " days.

Early Morning Love

It's early in the morning just about dawn
Wake up, Baby, let's have a little fun.
I'll be the hand; you be the glove
Wake up, Baby, let's make a little love.
It's not too early, I can see daylight
Plus we might as well start the day off right!

I got to get up in a minute and so do you.
Roll over right here, let's do our do.
Loving in the morning is the greatest thing
We can take our time 'til the alarm clock ring

Kissing and a hugging all the while
Damn but you know how to make me smile.
This feeling's so good, we gotta make it last
Slow down, Mama, we're getting a little too fast!

Slow down, Baby, we still got some time
Let other things flow through your mind
Like what you gonna buy when you go to the store
Wasn't there somewhere else that you wanted to go?

Didn't we talk to your folks last night on the phone?
There, that's it! I was almost gone.
Girl, you know you're my woman, and I know I'm your man
Doing all this good loving as only we can
Just me and my key and you and your lock
Not a moment too soon- You, Me and the alarm clock.
Ringgggggggggg!!!

BETTYE DELOACH PRESLEY

Back in the Day
(Growing up in rural Eudora, Arkansas)

Back in the day when all's said and done
though things were different, we still had fun.
Honey, we did the "twist", the "mashed potatoes" and the "booga-loo", too
whether our shoes were old or spank brand new.

If the woman by herself had chill'en to feed,
everybody pitched in to supply their need.
She didn't have to worry from day to day
'cause everybody helped in some special way.

Greens grew wild everywhere 'round here;
going hungry was an uncommon fear.
We all ate good and we all lived long
claimed sound minds and bodies strong.

People loved people a whole lot more.
Most weren't concerned about evening a score.
Po' folks knew what po' folks need
and CARE was more frequent than selfish greed.

Having no paved streets brought dust to our door.
We dusted the furniture and dust mopped the floor.
Keeping things clean was never a choice.
In these situations, chill'en had no voice.

Used books from across town were passed off to us,
and we accepted them gladly without a fuss.
We never let the small things cause us to stray;
we studied and worked toward a brighter day.

We acted real good and tried hard to learn.
Getting a good education was a major concern.
If we misbehaved, we were scared to go home
'cause Mama nor Daddy would leave us alone.

There was no SCAN to interfere with their right.
Nobody to stop them from pulling our pants tight
and helping us to remember wrong from right
any time of the day and even at night.

And from our side of town grew professional breeds
Much farther advanced than some other folks seeds.
Who would have thought back in the day
That black folks would ever live in a much better way?

Like clockwork, the whistle blew at 9:00 Saturday night,
and all the black folks immediately took flight
to hurry back to the "black side" of town
to polish off the weekend by boogying down.

Church? Did you say church?
Chil', we had some church back in the day!
All of our deacons could sho' nuff pray.
Some prayed so hard they broke out in a sweat
just begging the Lord to forgive and forget.

'Cause back in the day some men played around,
but most of the wives felt duty bound
to teach their chill'en to respect their Dad
mainly because, he was all they had.

Some folks walked to church -- their shoes in a paper sack
with dust up to their ankles as they crossed the track.
"Certain folks" had cars but most did not
so some comfortable shoes really hit the spot.

We praised the Lord and shouted out loud,
no matter how large or small the crowd.
We thanked Him for all of the things that we had.
Regardless of our circumstances, we were mighty glad!

And Christmas was something we looked forward to.
If Santa was nice, we got something new
'cause times were tuff, way back then
but Christmas stayed Christmas to the very end.

So many changes since back in the day,
Yet no one dares to ask for an instant replay
'cause change is GOOD, and it must set in
or we're trapped in a vision of what might have been.

... But We Got Game

You bounce me freedom;
I bounce you confinement.

I bounce you honesty.
You bounce me dishonesty;

You bounce me mixed emotion;
I bounce you true devotion.

I bounce you unforgiveness.
You bounce me forgiveness;

You bounce me dispair;
I bounce you hope.

I bounce you all I got;
You bounce me what you got left.

You say it's the bounces.
I say it's the balls.

Damn, Dam

Damn, the dam broke in Orleans Parish.
Maybe but maybe not!!
Anyway, water got loose and took control of a whole city for days.
That was the day I learned to fear water, especially in volume.
And who took credit for the madness, devastation, and human suffering
A power hungry, fame seeking, self exalted Katrina.
But maybe it was the dam.
DAMN!!!!!

A Formal Thank You
(to both My "I Do's")

You were both special to me -- each in his own way.
Perhaps it was you who taught me to pray.
If that's not a reason to make you "dear,"
A better reason, I'd love to hear.

You two came into my life; each at a different time
and with a promise that seemed to match mine.
Neither too handsome nor built so fine
One commonality -- a taste for wine.

You taught me that alcohol was a foe to the free.
It kept both of you on a never ending spree.
It stifled your emotions and kept you weak
Denied you the opportunity to reach your peak!

You were the masters of bad habits, I have no doubt.
You slurped it up and blew it out!
Taking each day for granted without a clue
That all of your habits were killing you!

You taught me dishonesty and just how to lie.
You did it so easily; you didn't have to try!
You made good money but that was all;
maybe your minds were just too small.

"Unevenly yoked" is now clear to me.
In times passed, I refused to see.
Was it the blinders you put over my eyes
that kept me from seeing what I truly despise?

Thank you for so freely giving of your seed--
my daughter, my son, my biological need.
Two precious jewels came out of the deal;
the pangs of gratitude, I can actually feel.

I am personally indebted to both of you.
You've broadened my horizons, expanded my view.
You helped me to wake up from the helluva dream.
I'm so wide awake, you worked like a team!

You two guys have made me strong
and taught me endurance all day long.
Because of you, I can stand the test.
God knows I was taught by the very best!

With what you've taught me, I can treasure a storm,
come out of the cold, step into the warm
and sip so savorly the spice of life
without any malice, disdain or strife.

Thank You So Much!

Minds Gone Awry

A mere meeting of the minds ...
What minds?
Minds that exude bullets encrusted with criticism and fault finding.
Minds that think and act only to feather their own nest.
Narrow minds? Feeble minds? Minds that lead other minds?
Minds that never mind pitting one mind against another mind!

A mere meeting of the minds ...
All sorts of minds!!
Minds that promise yet seldom deliver.
Minds that conjure up lies to cover wrongdoings.
Creative minds? Manipulating minds? Hell raising minds?
Minds that twist the truth and cloak themselves with innocence!

A mere meeting of the minds...
A multiplicity of minds!!
Minds that delve deep into the human spirit only to misconceive
Minds that easily lose perspective in the run of a day.
Devious minds? Spiteful minds? Shallow minds?
Minds that work relentlessly to do a dirty deed or sow a rotten seed!

Indeed, a mere meeting of the minds...
Incredible minds!!
Minds intoxicated with the wine of jealousy and hypocrisy.
Minds dedicated to meeting!!!
For what?
complicating lives
designing upheaval
deterring progress
Why else would these minds dare to meet?

In His Likeness

Out of nowhere, she quirled, swirled and hurled her way into the Cresent City on assignment to steal, kill and destroy. And that she did!

Without remorse, she stole:
homes from hardworking families with no inkling of eminent destruction
schools from eager young minds curious to learn
hospitals from feeble bodies in search of refuge from sickness and disease.

In a violent rage, she killed:
people -- their bodies, their minds, their joys and even their dreams
all signs of live vegetation and unsuspecting wild life,
an economy, a way of life, a culture deeply rooted in relentless sin

And when she was done stealing and killing, she began destroying.

With one powerful gut-wrenching blow, she smote:
churches
businesses
institutions and everything else that was left.

Maybe no one else did, but I recognized her the moment I saw her.
I could tell by the way she hissed and slithered around the area
like an oversized Anaconda reeking with deception and infamy.

Perceptive eyes like mine could see the vicious she devil Katrina,
a carefully crafted facsimile of Satan himself, meticulously fashioned
--in his likeness.

Here's to the Red, Black and Green !!!
(a black history poem)

My heart belongs to the **red**, black and **green** --
A different flag from the one you've seen.

There's a special message attached to this flag
Believe me, it's not just a colored rag!

The **blood** of my people is the color **red**;
No distinction among them -- the living nor the dead.

The **black**, please remember, colors **our face**
To be black and proud is no disgrace!

The **land** our ancestors worked was covered with **green**;
Looking out over the fields -- a beautiful sight to be seen!

Yes, my heart belongs to the **red**, **black** and **green**!
The **blood**, the **people**, the **land**
The flag for which my people stand!!

Our people are the people who shed the **blood**, and
worked the **land** and stood boldly together **hand in hand**.

But Was It Ever Really Lost?
(My Take on Beauty)

Once, I found beauty in nature
When I *beheld* it **in** *an array of autumn leaves and pretty green grass*
Blanketing the hillside on a summer day.

And I found it *in a quiet room*
When I *caught a glimpse* of "The Mona Lisa"
Hanging majestically over the fireplace.

And yes, I found it *in a private and intimate moment*
When I *watched* as they shared the beauty of true love
Experiencing its awesomeness day after day.

I found it once more
when I *looked* toward heaven and *viewed* it **in the colors of a rainbow**
Shrewn so perfectly across what one day was a troubled sky.

Early one Saturday morning, I found it **in my flower garden**
As I *gazed* at the petals of a gorgeous yellow rose unfurling
Slowly right before my eyes.

In August of 2002, I found it **in the delivery room** at Chicot
    Memorial Hospital
As I *peered* from behind half closed eyes to witness the birth of a child.
Ah, the beauty of human life!

Many years ago, I found it **on the winding path** to Mama Ivory's house
As I *peeked* around each curve
That brought me closer to my grandma's arms..

Finally, I found it lying unnoticed **on the counter at the travel agent**
When I *laid eyes on* two enticing brochures
Exhibiting the beauty of Aruba, St. Croix and the Virgin Isles during
    vacation time.

Without searching, I found beauty almost everywhere
Not lost -- but nestling quietly **in the recesses of my mind**
Waiting patiently for the opportunity to present itself.

Sweet Solace

(to my friend "Sister" who died in Mt. Morris, Michigan)

There she sits on the edge
of a frayed carpet in a corner in the dark
basting in the grief of the loss
of her dearest and closest friend.

Grief has engulfed her much like
a mighty fortress claiming her full attention
but she does not fret; she writes
a poem for Willa. Her god-given gift
once again rescues her from the agony
imposed by the cessation of life.

She is empowered to express
a myriad of emotions through freestyle
and verse. Just writing the poem brings
solace to the experience and makes
it so much easier to bear.

She is at peace within the confines
of her space--the space reserved
for her and her most precious possession.

In this special corner, she is able to escape
some of the pain. She and her gift
blend together to bring the inside to
the outside creating the sweetest release.

Together they fondle words causing them
to contort from one extreme to another
until they settle into the exact position
to express her innermost feelings.

Ideas encased in meaningful phrases and
clauses rush through her head voluntarily
desiring to serve her unselfishly as she
lifts her pen in desperation.

She is totally consumed by memories
that she and Willa have shared.
Though the experience gets harder
by the minute, she is comforted by
the spewing out of the verbal euphonies
that crowd her mind.

She will get through this -- no doubt.
Willa would have it no other way!!
These things she must record
not for Willa's sake but for her own;
lest she forget battles they fought
together or the perfect vacations
that they planned.

A poem for her closest friend must become
a collage of events, occasions, incidents
and situations that bonded the two of them

She must allow it to paint a picture of visual
images of the two of them as their lives
intermingled decade after decade.

This poem must speak more of happy
times, since happy times seem to linger
endlessly and bring fonder memories.

Alas! It is finished!
The tale has been told and Willa is gone,
still gone! Yet through the medium of
words, a heavy burden has been lifted,
a load has been lightened.

Having completed the last stanza,
the memory of her friend stands
boldly before her flashing like a neon
sign so bright that it makes an eternal
imprint that only poetry can afford a poet!

An Addict's Plea

Oh, infamous assailant:
My body begs for the certainty of affliction
as you appoint me a suitable prey.
Give aid to my impoverished spirit.
Uncontrollable cravings leave me
unsuspectingly drained
while my family and those who love me dearly
sit helplessly awaiting the inevitable.
You hold me captive!
I cringe from your powerful touch
yet I perish gradually
though at my own request.

The Absence of Light

Midnight falls on a black man
Wearing a black suit and a black hat
Driving a black limo
Down a black tarred road
Cluttered with black cats
In a world filled with black smoke

And he ponders where the light went!

Within

Doesn't real peace really begin
Deep in one's heart, deep down within?
If your heart is troubled,
for you there is no peace
until all your troubles begin to cease.

Can you actually find peace
when there's turmoil in you?
Misfortunes and problems
whatever you do? Get a grip on the pain
and find relief
from all your sorrows and troubles and grief.

It's then that you'll experience
the wonderful peace
that comes when battles and wars decrease.

This is the peace that savors the heart!

Mystified!!!

After the night,
the day

After the caring,
the sharing

After the promises,
the lies

After the questions,
the answers

After the beginning,
the end

What then?

The Magic of Words

One confused young writer with pen in hand
wrote out his song with language command.

The words he wrote took him to lyrical height
but the magic of words delayed his flight.

"our" became "hour"
and "see" became "sea"
"air" became "heir"
and "flee" became "flea"

The night progressed and eventually grew old
but the magic of words never ceased to unfold.

"flower" became "flour"
and "blue" became "blew"
"pair" became "pear"
and "two" became "too".

The confused young writer put down his pen
and waited for his nightmare to come to an end.

Take A Closer Look, Please

To those who are blessed to be able to learn,
could I this one message on your brainpan burn?
I'd like you to realize how blessed you are
and how you must never go so far
off the deep end following others along
some who are weak pretending to be strong.

You must learn to live life by standards of your own
for the seeds that you plant now in your future will be sown
and those who helped you to sow the wrong seed
will always disappear when you are in need.

Beware of those who look for you both day and night
who can't be comfortable when you're out of sight.
It sounds like a lie, but it's really quite true.
They have big plans in their minds for you.

They'll help you to wallow and stay on the ground
blocking you from whatever good could be found.
They'll stick by your side as you partner in crime
and kill themselves laughing when you lose every dime.

Misery loves company, haven't you heard?
These guys are miserable; you are free as a bird
but only if you wake up from the mess each stirs
before your own pain and misery occurs.

Say your goodbyes to the riff-raff, bid them ado!
Take a trip to the mirror and smile at your view.
Think to yourself, I am God's very own
into my life many blessings have been thrown.

Not because I deserve them but because I'm his child
and He is so merciful, so meek and so mild.
Speak words of praise right then and there.
Tell Him you love Him; Show Him you care.

Come over on the Lord's side before it's too late.
Satan and his imps could soon seal your fate.
Rendering you helpless with nowhere to run
Leading you to believe it's all done in fun.

You'll see some changes go on in your life;
your so called friends will conjure up strife.
They won't care to be around you any more;
consider yourself lucky they went out the door.

They could never do for you what my God can;
they have no knowledge of an upright man.
Neither do they want to see you do good
even if they feel that you probably should.

They were never in your corner; no, not at all.
They only wanted you to abandon the call
that has been on your life for quite some time.
Thank God you made it, and life's now sublime.

Visions

Up ahead there could be happiness.
You, me and a winding path
that takes us through
whatever life hurls our way.

You leaning on me; me leaning on you
weathering each storm together,
sharing the happiest moments of our lives,
smiling as each day brings us more peace and joy.

In the distance, we celebrate our passion.
Just the two of us snuggled in our own private world
affirming each others strengths; rejoicing at each others triumphs,
letting in only those who can contribute positively to our
continued bliss.

But as for now, there are only visions.
We merely set sights on the beginning of our times together.
Searching each incident, analyzing each situation, examining every possibility,
making futile attempts to determine whether it would be worth our while
or whether we should be as two ships passing in the night.

DEBRA ANN JASPER

My Sleepless Dream

While lying awake from dust to dawn
Contemplating my possible fate
I have tossed and turned in absolute despair
Praying changes wouldn't come too late.

I have soaked my pillows with millions of tears
Pondering situations I could not control
I have often stared off into space
Trying to grab a good strong hold

I have lain awake with eyes cast upward
Looking toward the Heavens above
Countless times I reassured my tortured soul
That we are anchored in God's true love

When times looked darkest I marched on
Often moving at lightning speed
For I knew if I ever slowed my pace
I would not get done the deed.

I realized the darkness in my life
was only a nightmare, just a dream
So I sat straight up in my bed
Because things were not as they seemed
I was having a sleepless dream.

I Want Love

I want love to take me in its arms
And ravish my inner being
Simply consume my soul and make me a willing captive

I want it to rush my brain stem
And take residence in my mind
Rule my desire and make me shed inhibitions

I need that wild free feeling
An "I don't care who knows it" attitude
I want love to saturate me, wash me down

Love has to come and rescue me from doubt
It will have to alleviate my ladylike manner
Make me an easy mark for the right man

I want to be like a bird in rapid flight for love
Going wherever it takes me
Doing whatever it dares me to do

Fear cannot be a problem in my love plan
I'll stand and let it own me
I need its order to move on or lie down

Come, love, walk the path of seduction with me
Have your way
Use me
because

I WANT LOVE!

Can Love Be Trusted?

I have learned not to trust love
Not to be consumed by it
Love is a deceptive emotion
To taste of love is sheer poison
To drink from love's cup
Is to sample liquid fire
To invite love in is to walk
hand in hand with death
A painful demise
A death of uncertainty
I observe love and lovers at a distance
To look closely can cause blindness
To touch can cause
irreversible paralysis of the mind and soul
You begin to get consumed
By trickery and illusion
You imagine love is real
Once the deceptive emotion enters your brain
It permeates to the heart and causes an attack
Foolish reactions occur with love
Faulty judgement sets in
You become trapped in a world of grandeur
An unbelievable infatuation
Run for your life
Run from love
It can Not be trusted!

The Fall

DOWN
DOWN
DOWN I WENT

THE FALL WAS TRAUMATIC
AND I WAS SPENT

BUT IT DID NOT STOP
I FELL SO FAR
I FELL ON TOP

UP
UP
UP I FLOATED
FEELING BLOATED

BUT WHO TAKES THE BLAME FOR THE FALL?

He'll Do It

When into my life the storm clouds roll
And into my mind Satan assumes control
When disappointment is my daily bread
   I take time out to clear my head.

I clear my head with words of prayer
Words that remove doubt Satan put there
   I ask the Lord to make me strong
I grab inner strength and try to hold on.

My prayer will be answered; this I know.
For the words in the Bible tell me so
When times look darkest and doubt clouds my view
I trust God to do what he said He would do.

When in my life doubt reserves a room
With indecision, fear, pain and gloom
I gather my will and think a good thought
I know my salvation has already been bought.

He'll do it - make a way out of no way
He'll do it - bring the sun and take the rain away
He'll do it - make you strong in your weakest hour
   He'll do it -- He can--He's got the power!

Oh, Katrina

She came in with the force of ten NFL teams
Destroying life, hope and all future dreams.
The destruction was atrocious to the human eye.
Why did all those people suddenly have to die?

The fury was uncontrollable, the devastation complete
Sheer terror and torment ravaged each city street.
No one was protected neither by color or by age
No one could challenge Katrina's rage

She rained down disaster like a summer shower
People drowned and were thrown about by her power
For days upon days the city stood still
New Orleans bowed down to Katrina's will.

The Cresent City of Mardi Gras and party nights
Went for months and months with no parties and no lights.
The French Quarters and Bourbon Street were all in her quake
And were taken down fiercely with a force and a shake.

She came to New Orleans with the force of ten NFL teams
Ripping the Cresent City apart at the seams.
There's an eerie stillness in and around the Superdome
One day the remaining citizens may get to go home.

It Doesn't Matter

You can talk about me and beat me down
Lie on me, turn my smile into a frown
But whatever you do for the harm of my soul
Will be returned to you double fold.

You can hate me, abuse me, even laugh at my pain
But I'll keep on trucking through the storm and the rain
What is done intentionally to break my heart
Shall be returned to you, every part.

You can laugh when I'm hungry or grin when I'm broke
But what goes around comes around is not a mere joke
Because whatever you do to destroy my good name
Is like Russian Roulette--it's a dangerous game!

You can show jealousy and inflate my faults
But the Good Lord knows all of your thoughts
Whatever you do to cause me disdain
Is like a planted seed; it's coming up again.

You can smile in my face pretending to be my friend
Showing false concern to the bitter end
Whatever you do to confuse my mind
Is a solvable problem corrected in God's time.

So go ahead try and confuse my mind, cause me disdain,
destroy my good name, break my heart,
You can even try and do harm to my soul
Because whatever you do -- comes right back to you!

My Soul As A Lookout

My body and soul stood on the brink of tomorrow
catching a glimpse of yesterday.
My body turned, I had seen enough.
Father Time said' "Don't leave, stay."
Why should I stay? I've seen it all.
I see all I need to know.
"You saw convenience not reality;"
"let your soul stay, don't go."

Okay, maybe another minute,
we might even stay two,
but there are millions of important things
that my soul and I have to do.
"What is more important," asked Father Time
"than looking back and understanding?"
"I live for the future," I muttered,
"and could you be a little less demanding?"

"The future is looked forward to;
the past has already been,
but I believe it would humble you somewhat
to revisit the past again."
Alright, alright if it would make you happy
let's revisit what you said we didn't see.
He took my hand, I started to spin
My soul, Father Time and me.

I saw death in war torn Iraq
Africa ravaged by AIDS, Oh, sweet Mother Land
I couldn't imagine such devastation
Now, my soul, too held tightly to my hand.

Starving babies held each other close in Sudan
Eastern countries made young girls sex slaves.
"What in the world is going on?" I asked
when I saw people living in caves.
I looked at my soul, and I thanked Father Time
for helping me realize what the look back was about
And every since that miraculous journey
My soul has been my lookout.

Things I Like In People

People who acknowledge that God is real
Who work each day instead of steal
Who avoid a scam for the legitimate deal
Who enjoy a well cooked and enticing meal.

People who praise God and give him their all
Who don't procrastinate or drop the ball
Who heed the warning and answer the call
Who bravely get up each time they fall.

People who do unto others as they want done
Who take life seriously yet have a little fun
Who get in the race and win the run
Who reach for the stars, the moon and the sun.

People whom you believe you can trust
Who admit they have had a sexual lust
Who voice opinions and display disgust
Who get things done because they must.

People who aren't afraid to bear the soul
Who can play the game and assume control
Who have ferocity and can be bold
Who set the mark and meet the goal.

Those are the things that I like in people!

First Lady Rosa Parks

She lay in state at the Rotunda
Making history even in death
The course of the South had been changed by Rosa
As for her accomplishments, she had none left.

Rosa left an immortal legacy
to the cause of fair and right
The race torn South learned a solid lesson
They learned that the underdog has fight.

She'd worked hard that day and her feet were tired
All she wanted to do was sit down
But old Jim Crow raised his racist head
And turned the state of Alabama around

It was a crucial time and frightening as well
But still Rosa Parks claimed her stand
The entire nation was in shock and surprised
at the persistence of the black woman and the white man.

Who was he to demand that a woman stand up
And give him her seat to ride?
Her refusal changed those racist ways
Now the South has to take it in stride.

As Martin King came to her aid
The Civil Rights Movement was conceived
And all those honors that our ancestors dreamed of
Have become reality and can now be believed.

Thank you First Lady Rosa Parks!

You Just Can't Tell

You can't judge a book by its cover
But you can read the writing on the wall
When trying to parade through this slippery life
You must always get up from the fall.

You can't judge a person by the mistakes that they make
But you can gather their sense of pride
For mistakes are the process by which we grow
As we take what life offers in stride.

You can't really tell a person's worth
By the phony words that tumble about
Better that you judge a person by actions
That's the real person no doubt

You can't judge a book by its cover
You must learn to turn the right pages
For it is sometimes what is never said
That causes confusion through the ages.

So let's not read the cover
Without reading the entire book
Let's not give one short glance
But give life a long hard look.

Never assume what happens
Always be persistent and know
That what we think is a peaceful situation
Sometimes steals the show.

Because you just can't tell!

A Prayer To My Father

Now Lord, please hear me as I pray
Continue to guide me everyday
Look past my faults -- you know my needs,
excuse my bad, let me sow good deeds

Lord, I praise you as Maker of all.
You are my cushion whenever I fall.
You stand by me daily, it's you that I trust
because you are forgiving, loving and just.

In life as I blunder, I too shall forgive
It's the Christian way--the right way to live
I pray for my people going down the wrong track
I ask you Dear Lord to please guide them back

Now Lord, please hear me as I silently pray.
You watch over me all night as down I lay.
I pray for people walking down the wrong road;
deliver them, Lord, and lighten their load.

Lord, I lift you higher and higher in praise,
Feeling unconditional love and mimicking your ways.
Drugs are rampant and drive-bys are sure
You Lord, are the only one - divine and pure.

Your purity is seen in the beauty of the flowers
You give us time- seconds, minutes and hours.
Even the birds of the air take heed to your call.
You set the sun, hung the moon, Lord, you did it all.

As one of your children, Father, I thank you so much
for the wonderous gift of life and your tender touch.
Lord, I will sing your praises one million ways
and honor you, Father, for the rest of my days.

Poetry To The Poet

Poetry is intercourse with the soul
A look taken with an impartial view.
This look is given each time a poet writes
A carefully chosen word or two.

To peer into the soul can be a scary situation
You never know what thoughts lurk within.
But it is undeniable that you get a peek
Each time a poet grasps a pen.

Poetry -- an acceptable answer to a confused world
The poet imagines a lost and twisted situation
Poetry consists of love, lust and corruption
and are joined by great pain and humiliation.

Come in to unlock the hollows of my mind
That closed door to joy and pain.
Life offers challenges requiring monumental decisions
You can acquaint yourself with loss and gain.

If the mind is truly a terrible entity to waste
Then all thoughts should be untouched and clear
But that idea defies human reality
Evil and hatred tend to visit courting disaster and fear.

Poetry is an outlet to subconscious confession
The id, the ego and the inner Me
Back up your range of vision and see my self-made show
It is an uncharged look. There is no workable fee.

The unexplained and the unattainable
All of these thoughts knock at my door
My mind has to ability to vacation anywhere
And still my range gets higher. I reach for more.

The words become jumbled, they rattle about
Sometimes they emerge in my sleep.
Poetry to the poet is intercourse with the soul
As emotions begin to slowly creep --from my mind.

Dna

The blood flowed through my veins with awesome rage
Our love was dead; I didn't need to read this page
I couldn't believe that it was actually him standing there
But there he stood across from me, like he didn't have a care.

I didn't need to reminisce how I'd wished he was dead
As I faced the moment, I needed to clear my head.
After my Daddy died, he left me and my whole world simply fell
All I needed to say to him was "Boy, go straight to Hell".

A beautiful, healthy son was born and entrusted to us
What I envisioned as true love was merely animal lust
He took my self esteem and destroyed all my trust
My interpretation of him? He could go back to the dust.

My college sweetheart, my lover, my facsimile of a friend
He lied when he said he'd be there through thick and thin
He cheated on me with a new chick and a cheap bottle of gin
He even missed his son's life, how immoral, what a sin!

The blood flowed through my veins now at a normal beat
I stared straight into his eyes then looked down at his feet
I knew this day would come; we would have to meet
His face looked worn, his hair was thinning but he was dressed fairly neat .

With fiery eyes I had the courage to look directly into his face
I needed to start the conversation and keep it at my pace
"You started this marathon in my life, but I have won the race"
He was stunned by my words; they were like a can of mace.

"How are you?" I asked as I stood straight and proud
He hesitated looking sad before crying aloud
"I was afraid to come to you and stand up and be a dad
Now that I actually hear the words, it all is kind of sad."

"I have no vindication to ease the torment in your mind
What you did to our three lives was cruel and unkind
But fret not, my son, I didn't go through life blind
Let's revisit the life you missed, put it on rewind

You made me the strong woman that I am as we speak
I guess I owe you thanks; I learned never to be weak
See, after you left me with a son to raise
I prayed to God in Heaven for so many better days.

I learned to be a good mother and an equally good dad
It was a hard double role but now I am so glad
That I raised a baby boy who can take the good with the bad
Now he's a real man; he learned to use what he had.

Our son grew up to be a fine young man and quite responsible, too
See, he has a wife and baby; he didn't do like you.
He stepped up to the plate and got his education
He stood by his college sweetheart and ignored the temptation

Now if he allows you the privilege to be a part of his world
Be a good granddad to his sweet little girl
That's all I can tell you, all I have to say
You were a damn good example of bad DNA

The Eyes of a Child: Innocent Eyes

When I was a child,
I played in the yard
laughing and jumping;
I was so active
My heart double thumping,
I jumped in the dirt pile
For I viewed life
through the eyes of a child.

I drank root beer sodas
and ate lots of candy
I knew no problems
my life was just dandy
My grandparents were unreal
they made everything right
So I could snuggle in bed
and sleep safely at night
while I viewed life
through the eyes of a child.

My friends would sleep over,
I cheered at the games
I threw rocks at boys
and called them bad names
All was well at my house;
my life was set
because fear and adversity,
I hadn't seen yet.
I went to the prom;
I was dressed in style
That was all that mattered
through the eyes of a child.

When I started college,
I made the run,
met new friends,
had lots of fun.
But as time went on,
reality hit
Looking through a child's eyes
made me squint a bit.

I got into trouble;
I was bad for a while
but I still viewed life
through the eyes of a child.

I've made mistakes;
the list is quite long
I've done lots of good,
but I've done some wrong.
I've been up and down
and done it all
It's how many times you rise,
not the number of times you fall.

Now I look at life
in a different style.
I no longer view life
through the eyes of a child.
but I had to go back,
sharpen the file,
and attempt one last look
through the eyes of a child.

Through the eyes of a child
much power is given:
the power to dream the undreamable
the power to reach for the unattainable
the power to be free spirits

Through the eyes of a child,
there is untouched love:
love for family, for teachers,
love for friends and a supernatural
love for life itself.

Through the eyes of a child,
there is complete trust:
trust that we will create
a safe world for them
and their future families
trust that we will care for them
and teach them to be productive
citizens in this our world.

So maybe every once in a while
we should all take a look
through the eyes of a child.

Evolving Love

**Love is an abstract emotion
Fueled by a potion
It's sexy and wet
You will never forget
LUSTFUL LOVE**

Love is painful and fiercely cruel
It is under one rule
It is absurd and demeaning
Leaves you steaming
JEALOUS LOVE

Love is to come when I call
Or I don't need it at all
It is pleasant when it pleases
And fun when it teases
CAREFREE LOVE

Love is tender and meek
It makes your knees weak
It is caring and real
And it cares how you feel
REAL LOVE

Love can be **LUSTFUL, JEALOUS, CAREFREE** and **REAL**
It all depends on how you feel

CHARLES MEREDITH

Take This As A Lovepoem

in the afternoons
you sprawl in shafted sun
distinguished by deities of smiles
where, on occasion
you become uprooted,
no strength to resist
two personal sides of a dream.

it hasn't always been sawdust and sun.
it hasn't always been such a light.

take this as a lovepoem
use it gently,
then make of it garnish.

make mention that i did bring some sun

as i came monsooned and sure,
speaking in mixed tongues
making insane wishes
that canvass thoughts or meditate minds.

i wish for you
a talisman of evenings
that brightens and moves off,
making paradox
those questions you make poetry of.

A Ruck Of This And That
(for Lorraine)

to copy the same words each day
and then rewrite again
can never be gladly good,

it is a challenge
or a fitful delirium at best.

there is something to be said
of being young and footloose
taking everything
by dash
and nothing by
decision.
it can never be easy,
each day a rue, a munch of pain,
a ruck of this and that.

it is audacious if anything
trying to turn away all laidout plans
or sweated wishes.

they are necessary
as well as frail and fuzzy

and, just like
a phoenix unraveling
shifting and resurrecting
itself from its own ashes,

will reward much.

I Love To Love

I love to love and be love and
have love and get love and do love
and taste love

gently savor the feel of love

even dip love like a good snuff,
it's not that I'm so romantic or so erotic
or want to make a good impression,
I just love to
love.

A Saintified Church Meetin In Lakeport, Arkansas

come ovah heah,
de table spread/
come ovah heah,
de table spread/
oh, oh come ovah heah...
young rev. clyde strutted
a nice good sermon,
hallelujahs richocheted off
concrete floors,
block walls trembled
as angels hugged
fourcorners and wondered,
my breath, a reprobated armor,
was cut short as i searched each
soul and played their faces.

jagged praises sailed
toward the morning star
while uncertain thomases
mimicked the spirit.

as each plea of forgiveness
did vibrate and simmer to
discreet glory,
i gazed at the angels
with heavenwiped smiles,
i noticed the demons
with starving eyes
and wondered,
can these be my people,
can these be the people
that's going home?

After Hearing The Call For Participants In The Million-man March

    come,
    this is the wish. unite.
    come decently rough. strong.
    speak exact
    in blackist tones.
    not gobbledygook not painted phrases
    that work thru readycut places.

    forge a caucus of men, of guru-men.
    rekindle a spirit of walkingstraight-men.

    come. stand shoulder to shoulder.
    come. with a somewhat looping walk,
    however. come. unite.

For You Maurice, To Read When You Can
(my godson at 7 months)

it's limber legs and gerberstuff right now,

twitterly-thump, twitterly-thump, twitterly-thump-thump

but it will be clear soon
or late that you
always crawl
and then walk.

little hand-man and tinkling ball
are stunning
and in a hurry
are fumbling joy and toddlerfuss,
and you a little handy-man with miltonbradleykeys
listen and know
all keys do not open the silverdoors.

finding that
your little keys don't fit the doors
will really try you will disturb
your babysense.

there will be closed doors a plenty
with nofitting keys.

take a crawling start
and reach
the bowlegged balloonman,
bang his head
between the chairs,

scamper haphazardly among the youbetternots
and reshuffle a feeling here or there.

and
when you lug and lag
across the resisting floor,
when you finally explore the mazelike line,

when you do this,
then you will be walking.

twitterly-thump, twitterly-thump-thump-thump.

Poeticnotions

the poet takes a pen silently
& scribbles himself
    on
     a
piece
of notebook paper/
even make rime &
let   out
  imprisoned
thoughts
he must see very soon
poetic tycoon/
if he doesn't stop
replacing
hissoul with ink
won't be a space for tangled dreams.
won't be a place for stifled wishes.

sure wld seem funny/
saturated
on notebook paper.

he takes a pen silently
and
    implies   a change
    begs   a change
    demands   a change
even
    infuses   a change
yet
those who read will not understand
those who look will not see
those who listen will not hear
these
necessary
notions,
they will not look straightforward
to see
on his poeticface a strained,
anxious expression.

sure wld seem funny/
saturated
on notebook paper.

Sharing Forever

(to Al & Carolyn, for the child they want to have,
and in place of the poem that came too late.)

Sharing forever
a celebration
whether it be pink ribbons
or blue shawl,

there is love.

will you take the seventh door
or wait and grab
this babyish gift and splendor.
no need to rush
swindle or sweat,

there will be love.

in your mind
make prints of a small face
and share the eyes the frowns the wrinkles
the dimpled cheeks,
or spin rainbows of pink and blue
where at the ends is your gold,
and you are gold searching.
and you are better now.

on a moment
there is a smile
or an out-stretched finger
take it
play "patty-cake, patty-cake" and laugh.
and know

there will be a lovely love

to share forever.

For A Daddy Who Straightway Ran To A Bigger Place And More Space

that whiskied music
i know, was just like spanishfly
as yu cuddled in velvet nite,
ears against insecure riddles;
shy and grated answers
across brass bedsprings.
hands intoxicated and mov
ing without will,
it wasn't a gathering
of iron headed fellows,
yu were timidly in love
yor mind was reaching out
beyond repeated patterns,
but:
in watery boots and satin pants
yu went away
and mama decayed,
she died.

I Expect To See Him

i expect to see Him
any day now
a full force coming
ezekielfashion in a wheel.

i expect fire and beryl lights

as His glory descends suddenly
in a flame or cloud

in the quick of a thought
on the flash of a dream.

a slantwise stir
causing veils to fall as myths or voodoo,
causing a search and scream
for rock : fire : death : or any shelter.

i expect to witness a rapturingsky
that leaves lovers' arms empty
and cars without drivers.
causing collisions : confusion : and flabbergastic
praying to the god of the moment,
forgetting allah : buddha : and the other holyfellows.

i expect to see Him
as everybelievingone changes without warning
a new form formed (immortal).
for some, a loss of rewards.

at the seventieth week,

i expect to see Him
coming on the clouds of the sky
with power and great glory.

Beauty And The Beholder

They say beauty is
in the eyes of the beholder.

I passed by the beholder this morning,
I nodded my head & waved.
The beholder didn't wave back,
didn't nod back,
didn't acknowledge my presence.

Why didn't *they* see,
Why didn't *I* see,
The beholder is blind.

Conductor Of The Chinaman-store Bench

they say there's a lot of wisdom there, they say.
the conversations are finely spaced
between puffs of princealbertsmoke
carrying the squalor or luxury
of the tree-slab furniture
swirling through the air,
and the one-eyed dog
lay in silent stupor
as if he knows some terrible secret.

there always seems to be a conductor
or serious guru of this sitting place.

and it is very much an island
from the piss-musked alleys and doorsteps
leading from dim lit jukehouses
and the seductive
fast walking bodywords
of red-lipped swayish women.

the women of the town say they are all mad,
the benchsitters,
they sit all day and sprawl
out their sermons
how they had their ups and downs,
throwing their hands
in an oratory manner
as if to shoo a fly
or stress a fact about
the people on the other side of the tracks,
about the everySunday churchgoers
or the ticket giver at the edge of town.

one of them
seems to talk louder than the others,
seems to be uncouth
with his talking.
he must be the conductor.

You Know, I've Never Read A Marriage Poem

It's a sham
this til death do us part stuff,
what He joins together
is quickly put asunder.

you know, i've never read a marriage poem.

maybe it's taboo
or just not lyrical,
the weddingmarch and hymn.

i have never, never read a marriage poem,

nor was politely shown
a book of lace and linen

where emotions
are securely written
or where the bride instead
of the groom has become
a nervous wreck.

you know, i have never read a marriage poem.

the cautious vows.
the solitudal bliss.

i would just like to read a marriage poem
or so,

that can
touch and have its way
without all the nicks and nacks,
and be daggerperfect
in its intimacy.

Across The Tracks, On Armstrong Street

Behind the dancing place,
in front of Miss Hammie's café
sitting across the street from Bob Carr's gas station,
there is a motion starting up, a standing,
a rushing from a backyard, an alley,
a foot-trail leading to Gee Chinaman's
Grocery and chicken-seed sack-bar
where old lady Julia Barnett drinks her
Saturday ritual of beer to be ready
for the Mother's Board in a prime and proper
white starched dress come Sunday morning.

Speaking of Sunday morning;

the feather-filled tick and pillows
stuffed with cotton and out-grown clothes
seem to be snugger than usual
as the rain pellets play a constant tune
on the sheets of tin above the bedroom's
secluded darkness.
as you lay and think about
what it is you need from Hunter Walls' store
and how you will get there to get it,
there's no buses, no streetcars, no SEAT vans,
but there is H. Nichol's Taxi Service.

However, you think how you will need these 2 bits
to see the movie you always wanted to see
at the Eudora Main Street Movie Theater. you want to see this movie
even though you know you must sit up in the balcony.

It's Sunday night in the balcony.

The colored balcony, the apartheid balcony.
the balcony that smothers the effort you make
to get up Monday morning.
to dash out Monday morning.
to head out Monday morning to claim
your places at the Dermott Groceries Company
and the Dr. Pepper plant at the northwest end of town.

Then, there's Armstrong Street, Saturday night.
a spruced-up dream. a willing substitute.
the laugh and dance of many stifled lives
of those who survived in Eudora
back in the day, across the tracks.

I Think You Should Pull Your Hair Straight Back

I think you should pull your
hair straight back
and not be daunted
by the fact
that weekends only last 2 days
(I am always there)
there when you pull
your body onto mine
in topsy twirly tremble
causing love
to make a giddy sound
(slish slosh)
I am there
having you to laugh with
you to smile tippy-toe
in purple rooms with
or should I say red
(love is always red)
or maybe love is given
in shades of jasmine
and delicately crystal pleated
with multi-stitched polyester
I weave around
every nook and cranny
of your smile
reminding you that I
will always be there
that just like Chaka Khan, I really mean it
when I say
" I feel for you"

WILLIEFENE SYKES FORD

Rebuttal

(written in response to "I Think You Should Pull Your Hair Straight Back")

If I would pull my hair straight back,
  could you guarantee me the best
    two days of my life?
      or
  would I regret
    having wasted my time
      on a body not in twine with mine?

Yet
  you are there
    and
  I am here
at two different times --
  laughing - yes
But together
  or
  separately
about
  well, you know,
about the redness
    that should have been in the room
      but somehow didn't exist.

So with a smile on my face --
I will remember you,

For I feel for you, too.

Wise Up, Black Man

Get it together, Black Man;
rise up while you can.

You can no longer beat her down
and hold her ambitions to the ground.

She now can make it on her own.
She doesn't have to have you in her home.

The days are gone when you were in control;
for women now are truly quite bold.

Your money now doesn't mean a thing.
She can buy her own diamond ring.

You don't have to keep food on the table;
for with her own check, she is able.

You can't hold her down with a child.
She has become wise, though she remained mild.

Why try to hold her down with abuse?
You're only playing with a short term fuse.

You'd better not turn your back;
for she might might have what she used to lacka

So, Black Man, do get wise!
BECAUSE Black Women have begun to rise!!!!!

Psychotic Intoxication

    I walk in
        unnoticed
  like a fly on the wall.

     I stand
        not seen
  even though I'm quite tall.

     I sit
    alone
with no one at all.

I stare
       continuously
  as others have a ball.

     I stand
    leaving
ignoring their call.

I leave
      staggering
  about to fall.

    I wonder
      seriously
how I had the gall

        to even show up here at all.

Mesmerized

You put me under your spell
A thing you did so well.

You dangled before me a key
Put blinders on me so I couldn't see1

Down a lonely road you led me.
You simply refused to set me free.

Like a happy child I followed
And in your dirt I wallowed!

Though voices within said I was wrong,
You sang to me such a sweet song.

It made it hard for me to think
No matter how low you made me sink.

My conscious mind, I refused to hear
Even though my heart had a tidbit of fear.

I seemed to have lost control.
In fact, I lost my very soul.

You had me completely under your spell,
And you led me straight to a burning hell.

Weak Women

Weak women
Roaming the street
Smiling at every man they meet
Trying hard to get a date
Knowing some men just don't rate!

Weak women
Grasping for straws
Attempting to dodge all kinds of laws
Knowing that if they're taken in
They'll be forever committing sin!

Weak women
Running after other women's men
Men who don't care where they've been
Knowing all the time they just can't win!

Weak Women,
Figure you a better way out
All these men you can live without.

Life is just carrying you down!!!

The Gambler

He needs something to ease his mind,
so he goes out to make a find.

He never knows what danger he's in,
for he knows not where he has been.

He's the gambler who can't settle down
and he moves about all over town.

He gets whoever lets him in;
anybody who will let him win.

His life, he's putting on the line;
but he does not care; he feels just fine.

For awhile, he flies very, very high;
but soon his good times will surely die.

For if to many times he gambles,
his life will wing up in shambles!

We Need To …

We need to be strong
to make it further up the road.
We need to cast down
our weatherbeaten heavy load.

We need to face our problems
that will not go away.
We need to lift our hearts and begin to pray.

We need to cast not a single blame
That could keep others from finding fame.

We need to on certain issues speak
if the words we utter will help the weak.

We need to stand up and be brave.
It might mean many a life we save.

We need to walk the straight hard path
And never about others' misfortunes laugh.

We need to be strong
and sing our own song.

We need to be strong!

Despite the Facts

They kept us back
They said we couldn't read.
They beat our teachers
and hid our books.

But we moved on!

We found the books
that they had taken.
We studied hard.
We wanted success.

So we moved on!

When the freedom train came,
we gladly boarded.
It was a hard road.

But we moved on!

Yes, we were beaten
and sometimes killed,
but we were motivated still.

That propelled us as we moved on!

Now life is better
but not complete,
but we won't stop.
We will forever

Move On!!!

Don't Ask Me to Leave

Please don't ask me to leave
when I have just started in myself to believe.

I lived so long in the dark not knowing up from down.
Now I feel like I'm upward bound.

Don't ask me to leave now
before I give this world a bow.

I can see many works ahead,
and I'll get there before I'm dead.

I will open roads never paved
and change men never saved.

I will make a way for every man.
Something just tells me that I can.

Don't ask me to leave!
Let me do the things that I believe.

A Dead Slave's Prayerful Confession

I'm swinging on a tree, Lawd;
And I done did what you told me to do.
What went wrong, Lawd?
Did you not hear my prayer?
The one where I was begging you.

You said what I wanted, you would do.
All I wanted was to live,
and that I didn't get to do.

The sun that day got real hot,
and I couldn't pick an awful lot.

I tried, Lawd, but the heat made me weak,
and shade I had to seek.

I wasn't being lazy, Lawd;
but the heat made me crazy.

My head went round and round
and I fell upon that there ground.

I saw the overseer coming, Lawd;
and I heard the other's humming
    trying to warn me.

But I was sick, Lawd;
so I just took lick after lick.

He bruised me bad, Lawd;
he took away all the fight I had.

Then he tied me to his horse
and dragged to this tree.

He lifted me up with his bare hand;
and he said, "This is what you get
for not following my command."

But I was tired, Lawd;
I just wanted to go to sleep.

So now, I hang here dead
being held up by my head.

I have but one more thing to ask, Lawd.
Will you take me home, please
So I can take my rest?

I Can't Call It!

Now I can only stand and wait;
whatever happens is just my fate.

I can't begin to hasten my stay,
nor can I it delay.

Whatever comes I must face,
and I will do it at God's pace.

It won't matter if I stand alone.
For when I"m gone, I am gone!

Vain Labour

I tried to build a paradise
A place to call my own,
but life kept washing it away.
No inhibitions shown.

I tried again a paradise to build,
and I invited every friend.
Life loved my involvement,
for others I let in!

This was for sure a lesson learned;
you can't build a paradise alone.
Others must be in your life
to protect you from systems unknown.

No Friends

No friends:
    no sin
    nobody to let in
    nobody to defend
    nobody to help you win!

No friends:
    no one to relieve your mind
    no one to treat you kind
    no one to help you find
    no one to get you out of a bind.

No friends:
    nobody to call at night
    nobody to set you right
    nobody with whom to fight
    nobody to show you the light.

No friends:
    no one to be your guest
    no one to help you pass the test
    no one to show your cherished best
    no one to remind you that you need to rest

No friends:
    Nobody
        No one
    Nobody
        No one!!!!

I Praise the Man

I praise the man who stands tall
when being pushed against the wall.

I praise him who never gives in
when everything in life he can not win.

The one who good in others he continues to see
even when they refuse to let him be.

I praise him who loves all
and answers quickly to his call.

The one who will not let you down
when others fail to come around.

I praise the man who keeps going
when he knows and when he's unknowing.

He I know has a goal
and he has no plan to let it fold.

This man has a vision
and will surely make a fine decision.

He will not stop to rest
until he's passed the final test.

This is a man on whom we can depend.
A man who will always step right in.

For when this man does finally win
He'll halt to pull all of us in

I praise this man.
I PRAISE this man!!!!

The Men Of This World

Let me tell you a story about the world
and the people that give it its whirl.

From the poor man in the ghetto
to the rich man with his Stiletto.

The poor man is afraid
      because he may run out of bread;
Then his poor family will have no way to be fed.

The rich man is afraid
      because he has too much bread;
Yet he never has any to spare
To show others that he does care.

The poor man will stay in a shack
      and sleep on a croker sack,
for he never expects to have jack.

The rich man lives in a palace
      with rooms decorated in lace;
But he never invites the poor man in,
      for he thinks he might his palace deface.

But the poor man can work in the palace
    and keep the rooms all clean,
but he can't eat in the kitchen
    for he himself is still unclean

There's also the man in the middle of the road.
He carries the heaviest load.

For if he loses, he'll become poor
and can never again enter the rich man's door.

But one day, they all will die
and that we know is not a lie.

Then each will be put in the ground
Where there won't ever be a sound
and by the very same dirt,
they'll ALL be bound!!!

From the Side of the Road
(a cynic's view of "The House By the Side of the road")

I love living like a hermit
by myself all content--
let me live all drawn apart
to watch the stars from my own firmament.

let me live apart
where highways never run
so I might like a craftman create my own fun.

let me live far from the side of the road
and carry my own load.

let me live possibly in a forest deep
where one only seldom comes
so i may my own company keep.

i don't care if i ever see men good or bad
for friends for life, i never had.

so let me live far off the road
and carry my own load.

the men i see from my window pane
are running rabbits down the lane
they don't look for me nor i for them.

i live with my smiles
i live with my tears
i have lived by myself
for all these years.

so why should i worry about the strife of other men
when i can sit right here happily in my own den?

just let me stay far from the side of the road
and carry my own load.

i know of the meadows and mountains, too.
so long i've traveled them alone
so when i see a traveler there
i'm wishing that he'll soon be gone.

why weep with the strangers that pass in the night?
they never did anything to make my life bright.

so let me stay far from the side of the road
and carry my own load.

let me live in my house where the animals pass by
and all of the birds forever fly
they never give me a reason to cry
they just day after day fly on by.

so let me stay away from the likes of man
far from the side of the road
and continue to carry my own load.

The Struggles Of
The Real Poet

Being a real poet is a struggle.
Sometimes it's downright hard.
He's always searching
    for the right word
    the right rhyme
    the right meter
It's enough to drive him wild.

But he loves every minute
Every struggling minute
Every minute of the time.

He finds the words:
he jots them down --
But they're not right
they're out of place--
a new struggle begins--
    Should this be here?
    Should this be there?
Sometimes it seems too hard to bear.

BUT he's a poet.
He can't stop there.
He must go on to finish the game.
The struggle is not yet over
the rhyme
the meter
    all must be in place.
It must be good enough for him to face.

Writing poetry is a struggling game,
and he doesn't want imperfection
    to be his blame.

So he moves words around
    like checkers on a board
sometimes losing
    and
sometimes winning,
but he must go on.

The struggle has just begun.

Don't Give Up, Yet

Sister, there is still hope!
Not every man has turned to dope.

It is never too late for romance.
You just need to find another chance.

Every man you find is not a crook;
You just need to continue to look.

When you meet, there will be a reaction
That will cause a natural attraction.

You won't be able to keep your eyes away;
It'll seem as if they meet to stay.

You'll get a wild imagination;
to be followed by an instant sensation.

You'll always want him around
and you'll listen to his every sound.

That man just gave you a ray of hope.
He's hardly ready to up and elope.

It's Gone!!

Gone from us
That feeling
Where love once resided.

Gone from us
the connection
the attraction
the moments
that were once ours.

Moving on
to a new day
to a better tomorrow.

Moving on
but with remorse.

We can't find the feeling
that we left behind.

ABOUT THE AUTHORS

Guaranteed to Cut & Soothe was written by the members of Razors and Bandaids Poetry Guild birthed in Eudora, Arkansas on October, 2005.

The charter members of the guild include:

    Williefene Sykes Ford, Retired English Teacher
    Bettye DeLoach Presley, Retired English Teacher
    Charles Meredith, Retired Art Teacher
    Debra Ann Jasper, Retired Nurse
    Josh E. Johnson, Sr., Local Entrepreneur

Printed in the United States
66549LVS00004B/22-30